Exploring The Seven Churches Of Revelation

An In-Depth Study Of Each Church:

Their Strengths, Weaknesses and why it matters in our lives today.

Susan C Howell

Exploring the Seven Churches of Revelation
An In-Depth Study Of Each Church:
Their Strengths, Weaknesses and why it matters in our lives today.

Published by Vacations Unlimited Publishing
4091 De Zavala Road Suite 3
San Antonio, Texas 78249

ISBN 978-0-9862072-7-3

Unless individually notated, all Scriptures are taken from the Holy Bible, New King James Version (NKJV) Bible Gateway, on line.

Copyright@2015 by Susan C Howell

All rights reserved. No portion of this book may be reproduced, stored in a retrieval system, or transmitted in any form or by any means – electronic, mechanical, photocopy, recording or scanning without the prior written permission of the publisher.

Printed in the United States of America

2015 First Edition

This book is available for purchase in bulk or volume discounts when purchased by corporations, organizations and special-interest groups. Custom imprinting or excerpting is available to fit special needs. For information and pricing, please email: **susan@susanchowell.com**.

Due to the nature of this changing world, any locations mentioned in this book may have changed names since publication and may no longer exist by the names mentioned within.

My profound
Thanks to:

My husband;
David Howell for your love, ongoing spiritual covering and your prayers. And for always being my best friend.

Lisa Bonnet;
The faithfulness you have for our Lord, and your desire to share His BIG, BIG Word over me has blessed and encouraged me in ways that only He knows.

Zia Bingaman;
Your support and encouragement with all of my books and your love of Biblical history has been so encouraging.

Elizabeth Garcia;
I appreciate your eye for detail. Your loving correction is so greatly appreciated.

Introduction

Please read Revelation 1 - 3

I love to read God's Word. I feel the healing flow pour over my body. My muscles in my shoulders and back relax and my foggy brain is soothed, most of the time! Sometimes I read a passage or a sentence and my muscles tighten. I get frustrated because it doesn't make sense. The wording overlaps or runs in weird sentences.

I think of myself as a simple person; someone who likes easy to understand phrases. I believe that is why God asked me to share His word to the Seven Churches through my "simple eyes." He has such a clear message for each of us. I invite you to follow along with me as He takes us on a "simple" walk through the new churches. Planted and nurtured by John and Paul; men who walked step by step with Him in His ministry. Following His death and resurrection, they spread the Gospel in Asia Minor to the Gentiles and Jews alike.

John was the author of Revelation. Known as the Beloved disciple, he was with Jesus through His entire three year ministry. It is believed he is the only disciple who was not martyred for his faith and died at an old age.

Jesus loved John very much. He trusted him. When Jesus was on the cross, He trusted John with the responsibility of caring for His own mother: the woman who God had chosen to give birth to the Savior of the world. This woman knew at conception that her child was from God; she must have been incredibly proud of him as

He went about fulfilling prophesies taught to her from past generations. She was now watching her son suffer physical pain to the point of death. This very special woman Jesus gave to John to care for as his own mother.

Jesus knew that the revelation He was about to give John would be written correctly and completely. Whether John understood it or not, Jesus knew he would be faithful to do what was asked of him.

John was in his mid to late 20's when Jesus died. Mary was in her late 40's. He returned to Ephesus in 67 A.D. which meant he was about 65. Some religions believe Mary went with him, but that would have meant she would have been in her 80's. There is no proof she lived that long. There is only tradition that she was in Ephesus.

This book is the revelation OF, CONCERNING, and FROM Jesus Christ. God gave the revelation regarding the end times to Jesus, who, in turn revealed it to John through a vision.

Many people call this last book of the Bible "Revelations." It is only one Revelation. One complete, confusing at times, fascinating at others, yet only one revelation given by Jesus to John.

We all learn in different ways. Some can READ and understand completely, storing it away in total comprehension, while others learn by having it shown to them. Because we each learn, or gain clearer understanding in different ways, God reveals things to people differently.

My son-in-law is a reader. He fascinates me! He actually reads owners manuals and he understands them! I am a visual learner. If you give me a set of instructions on how to fix something, it will still be broken at the end of the day! I have a rough time comprehending written details.

If you take a few minutes and SHOW me how to do something it leaves a visual imprint on my brain which I can recall as needed. You may have noticed how I love visual descriptions, if you have read any of my other books, you know my love of details. I like those pictures!

This study is inspired by God. He spoke to me through my husband David telling me that I was to do this study for all of us - you and me - to have a clearer understanding of His word in each of our lives. We visited the Seven Church sites which are in modern day Turkey, to walk the streets, to learn the history of each community. To see what the towns were like and why Jesus said what He did to each of the churches. The pictures are taken by us for your clearer understanding of each city and church.

In the message Jesus gave to each church, you will find parts of yourself. God knows our weaknesses and He knows our strengths. The churches were the same as you and me...weaknesses and strengths. Some visible to the naked eye and some buried so deeply that only The Holy Spirit can see them.

Our goal with this study is to turn from the things that draw us away from God, back to those things that matter TO God. Each of the following weeks will take us to the different Churches in their unique towns. We will travel in the order in which the churches are on the Roman road, which is the order in which Jesus dictated them.

In the first century, the time right after Jesus resurrected and the disciples were spreading the Word, they were not called

Christians. The term at the time was: followers of "THE WAY." So when you read that term, it is reserved for the early Christians.

The letters John wrote would have arrived by boat from Patmos to Ephesus and made their way along the Roman road, in a counter-clockwise direction, which is the order in which they were given to John.

There are seven churches which Jesus spoke to specifically in the Book of Revelation; all are located in the region of Asia Minor. We know the area to be modern day Turkey, which is along the Aegean Sea in the western-most part of that country.

Notice how far Israel is from these cities. In modern times; travel from Jerusalem to the region of the Seven Churches by airplane takes over two hours. If you wanted to walk, it is over 1,700 miles and will take about 60 – 65 days, walking 8 hours each day and resting on the Sabbath. This was not a quick weekend get-a-way. It took time and planning to travel this far. Once a person was there, they needed to make the best use of their time.

Paul and John would have used donkeys as their main source of travel on their missionary journeys. They are more stable walking through the rough and mountainous terrain than camels and much safer than a boat. We know they did travel by boat, but it was not the safest unless one was confident the captain liked you. If not, he could choose to have you thrown overboard, keeping possessions and payment for the sailing.

WHO dictated the Book of Revelation and why?

Please read Revelation 1: 1- 11

It is clear Jesus Christ is communicating through His personal angel. He is the first and the last. He is the Alpha and the Omega. He uses many of the names attributed to the Son of God. The man we know as Jesus is the human part of the God-head. It is He who shed His blood on the cross for our sins.

Q Why am I interested in this study? _____
_____
_____

Q In Revelation 1:3 what does Jesus say we are? _____
_____
_____

Q Why is that important to me? _____
_____

Q Am I really ready to make changes as I uncover my weaknesses?_____
_____

EXPLORING THE SEVEN CHURCHES OF REVELATION

Q   Knowing that Paul and John traveled so far, would I be willing to make that trip in an air-conditioned vehicle, to touch the lives of others for Christ? _____ Why or why not?_____
_____
_____

Q   In chapter 1:17 Jesus laid His right hand on John and told him something that we should not do. What is it? _____
_____

Q   Is the love that Jesus had for John different than the love He has for you? _____ How?_____
_____

Q   Is there anything you can do to change His love for you?_____ How?_____

Q   If the Lord of the universe knew what was happening in each one of these churches, their trials and struggles, does He know my situation? _____

Q   Am I willing to let Him take care of the struggles?_____ How long (what length of time) are you willing give to Him, to "let" Him take care of the situation? _____
_____

Q   John could have ignored the task to write the Revelation. After all, he was in prison on a remote island. He allowed the Holy Spirit to lead him with such an important message for all generations. What are your thoughts about John?_____
_____
_____
_____

Q   Do I choose to ignore His promptings? _____ Why/why not?_____
_____
_____

EPHESUS

The Loveless Church

Please read Revelation 2:1-7

Ephesus was the capital of Asia Minor, one of the most influential cities in the eastern part of the Roman Empire. Once an important seaport with 250,000 citizens and 50,000 slaves, the ruins of the city now lie 5 miles from water. The temple to Artemis was one of the largest and most beautiful in the known world. It was located in Ephesus and provided a major industry for the community. They manufactured images of this goddess and her temple, selling them to locals, visitors and beyond.

As one of the three most influential cities in the Roman Empire, her ports operated twenty four hours a day. At night, a series of torches, or lamp stands, remained lit along the road leading from the city to the port.

Ephesus was a wealthy town with many huge homes built into the side of the hill. The homes have thousands of square feet of living space on multiple levels. Excavation has revealed examples of the wealth which existed here. Floors laid with tiny colorful stones forming mosaics over 15 feet in diameter. Frescos of blue, orange, green and mauve adorn the walls of most rooms and interior courtyards showing off the trappings of affluence.

Both Paul and John spent time here in Ephesus. Paul visited at least twice; living here for three years. When Paul wrote to the people here in Ephesus – the letter to the Ephesians – he wrote about things that many in our generation, 2000 years later, need to hear as well. He wrote about loving the family, focusing on Christ and turning from sin. His letter was directed to these people who had loved Jesus, yet they had slipped into the temptations that even modern man and woman are faced with. Today we struggle with keeping the focus on Jesus.

John's life work was to spread the good news of Jesus Christ and salvation through Him. Since he was living in the Roman occupied city of Ephesus under the rule of the Roman Emperor Domitian, he was bound by their laws. One of the laws forbids fortune telling, astrology and other cults. Christianity was considered in that category. As the Bishop of the church in Ephesus, he was told to stop teaching about Jesus. He did not. His punishment was to be shipped to Patmos which was a small Greek island reserved exclusively for prisoners, where he remained for several years. He returned to Ephesus where he later died.

Emperor Domination died in 96A.D. and Emperor Nerva took over. The new Emperor wanted to be the opposite of his predecessor; who was very mean and violent. One of the changes that Nerva did was to release scores of political prisoners, which he thought would show good faith and raise his level of respect throughout the empire. This is believed to be the reason John was returned to Ephesus; he was one of those released sometime during or after 96 A.D. John was in his mid 90's when he was sent to the island. It is believed he died around age 100 in Ephesus.

Let's look at each scripture and see what God wanted the people of Ephesus to learn.

***1** "To the angel of the church of Ephesus write, 'These things says He who holds the seven stars in His right hand, who walks in the midst of the seven golden lampstands:"*

Jesus describes himself here as holding the seven stars and standing in the midst of seven lamp stands. Jesus said in *Revelation 1:20 "The hidden meaning of the seven stars that you saw in the right hand and the seven gold lamp stands is this: The seven stars are the messengers of the seven churches, and the seven lamp stands are the seven churches."* Clearly this is Jesus Christ addressing the church in Ephesus.

Q How would you describe Jesus from this verse? _____
_____
_____

***2** "I know your works, your labor, your patience, and that you cannot bear those who are evil. And you have tested those who say they are apostles and are not, and have found them liars;"*

John spent much of his ministry in Ephesus and he knew that the faithful believers had resisted the false teachings. Paul also ministered in Ephesus and in his letter to them he warned the Ephesians about the imposters. Read Acts 20:29-31.

False teachers did indeed cause problems in the church, but the church resisted them as we can see from Paul's letter to them. The church in Ephesus had refused to tolerate sin among its members. This was not easy because of the immoral sexual practices associated with the goddess Artemis whose temple was the focal point of their city.

It was the central temple which occupied a large section of land. Beautiful to the eye, it was home to the temple prostitutes.

These ladies held an interesting position in the community. When the city held a celebration, there would be a parade. The temple prostitutes were the second group who walked in the parade. The first group was the senior adult men, known as the senators, or the aristocratic Ephesians. Everyone else followed behind the prostitutes. That should help to understand how far they had fallen.

In the second part of the verse, the early church recognized a select group of men who they called apostles. They were a very small and specific group who met three qualifications. 1. They must have been in Israel and had seen the man: Jesus Christ. 2. They had to be chosen by the Holy Spirit and 3. They had to perform signs and wonders which honored Jesus.

In this second verse of chapter 2, Jesus is commending the church for holding these men up to the test, to confirm if they truly were apostles. They claimed to be something they were not, and the church was faithful in casting them out. This was a very good thing!

Q   In what way did the first century Christians test men claiming to be apostles? _____
_____
_____

Q   In my personal life, how can I test the true spirit of men and women who claim to be Christian Leaders?_____
_____
_____

3 "and you have persevered and have patience, and have labored for My name's sake and have not become weary."

More than 24,000 people could sit in the theatre of Ephesus. On several of Paul's missionary trips to Asia Minor, he visited Ephesus. He and John knew the people and their problems quite well. During one of his visits, we read in Acts 19:23-41 about the uprising over Paul's teachings which came to a head in this theatre. The silversmith named Demetrius, who appeared to be a leader in the guild, and was a worker in silver, made shrines of Artemis. The entire silversmith gild accused Paul of ruining their trade by his preaching. They were a huge and quite powerful group. Its main source of income was creating trinkets and icons of the Greek goddess. As Paul preached, he educated the population that they did not need a piece of silver shaped into a human form to have God as their protector and provider.

A guild was similar to our present day unions or labor organizations. They held a tight grip on everyone who functioned in that industry. To be in a gild, one could not profess Jesus. This was a definite hardship on the families who chose Christ, and in this letter He wants them to understand that He understands their sacrifice to follow Him.

Q Jesus is complimenting the church of Ephesus here. What is He saying to you? _____
_____
_____

Q List a "hardship" you have dealt with over the years, and how God brought you through it. _____
_____
_____

4 *"Nevertheless I have this against you, that you have left your first love."*

As every good manager knows, you always tell your team

how much you appreciate their strengths before you have to tell them their shortcomings. Jesus has finished the strengths and now must address the church's lack of faith. When a person becomes a new Christian, they quickly fall deeply in love with Him. It is almost impossible to think or speak of anything except Him. Sadly, many in the church had lost that first love. They were "being Christians" without loving Him.

Q "Forsaken" means to abandon, reject or desert. Have I forsaken my first love? If so, what do I need to do to return to Him? If I have not, what am I doing to stay close to Him? _____
_____
_____

5 "Remember therefore from where you have fallen; repent and do the first works, or else I will come to you quickly and remove your lampstand from its place - unless you repent."

Oh! That first love of our Lord! How exciting and special it was. Do you remember it? John's writing here is reminding the church how far they have fallen out of love. How they have let "life" get in the way of their original love of God.

We all understand that we must repent, (turn from) our sin and fall back in love with Christ. The church in Ephesus was given a powerful warning. As a port city, it gained most of its wealth from shipping. A 40 foot wide marble street ran from the town to the dock. It's width was measured in Roman fashion: 20 Roman soldiers standing shoulder to shoulder. The length of this marble street was over 5 American football fields.

Shipping was a 24 hour, 7 day a week event, so tall lamp stands; (torches) were mounted on marble columns, placed on each side of the wide street to provide light. Without the light, they would not be able to work. Sadly, the Ephesians chose to work and not repent.

As Jesus walked this earth about 60 years before He gave this vision to John, He spoke in parables, or stories which the people to whom He was talking could understand. To a baker He talked about baking. To a fisherman, He talked about fishing. Now He is speaking through John to this church, He talks about their main industry: shipping. Ephesus sat on the Aegean Sea, which connects to the Mediterranean Sea. Ships came from as far away as Rome and Athens to fill their hulls with merchandise, much of which were the trinkets and idols of the silversmiths.

The Cayster River ran close to the city. It flowed 80 miles inland and was large enough to transport goods. Once they were taken off the large ocean-going ships which docked at the edge of town, they were transferred to the smaller vessels which took them inland to cities far from the sea. The church of Ephesus chose to ignore His warning, so the river began to bring silt into the harbor. Over time the ocean-going ships could not get to the dock because of the mud and eventually they quit trying to get their goods to and from Ephesus. Today, because of the mud buildup, the ocean is almost five miles from the "port" city of Ephesus. With no ships coming in, the lamp stands were not needed anymore. Jesus told them to repent or He would take away their lamp stands…and so He did.

Q What "lamp stand" could Jesus remove in my life if I do not choose to draw closer to Him? _____
_____
_____

Q Am I willing to risk loosing Him in exchange for keeping that "lamp stand" in my life? Why?_____
_____
_____

6 "But this you have, that you hate the deeds of the Nicolaitans, which I also hate."

The word "Nicolaitans" comes from the Greek word "Nikolaites." Which means "destruction, or conquer." The word "conquer" means to use force and control over someone. The Nicolaitans wanted to combine pagan worship with Christianity so they could control those who believed in Christ. Adultery, heresy, pagan idols in the home, were all encouraged in subtle ways. Anything that could cause division or divert one's focus and cause them to sin, yet look like they were believers.

This is what God hates. He hates people in authority ruling over, or controlling the lives of His people. Here in verse 6, He is giving the church a huge compliment because they hated the Nicolatians as much as He does.

Q In today's world, we do not call someone a "Nicolaitan" We use "politically correct" terms and encourage believers to focus on things not of God. What is there in my life that is drawing me away from a closer relationship with God? _____
_____
_____

***7** "He who has an ear, let him hear what the Spirit says to the churches. To him who overcomes I will give to eat from the tree of life, which is in the midst of the Paradise of God."*

Clear back in the first book of the Bible: Genesis 2:9, we find the term "tree of life." Adam and Eve were not told to stay away from it. They could eat from it as they chose because it was the embodiment of eternal life. Once Adam and Eve ate the forbidden fruit, through the other tree, "the tree of knowledge," sin entered the world. Man was no longer able to have access to eternal life until Jesus came and gave it to us. Now that "tree" is in the New Jerusalem, waiting for each of us. In verse 7 here, the faithful are encouraged to overcome; to have confidence they will eat from the tree of life in paradise.

Q Why does God want us to eat from the "tree of life," but not the "tree of good and evil?" _____
_____
_____
_____

Personal Notes

Columns in the Agora

A wealthy home. Notice the Mosaics on the floor and frescos on the wall

Theater which held 24,000 people

Harbor Street leading from town to the old port. The columns held torches allowing dock hands to work at night.

EXPLORING THE SEVEN CHURCHES OF REVELATION

SMYRNA

The Persecuted Church

Please read Revelation 2:8-11

As we read these verses, we don't see any reprimand or discipline as we did in Ephesus. Instead, there is acknowledgement of their struggles and their faith. We also read a great deal of encouragement and support of their faithfulness. No chastisement here.

Smyrna was another port city, like Ephesus. The town in general was a pretty rough crowd. Pagan worship was very popular, yet the city did not have huge pagan temples.

Jesus introduced Himself in this letter to the church in Smyrna as the first and the last, who died and came to life again. These are encouraging words to those in Smyrna who are suffering so much. They know that professing their faith will eventually lead to death. Yet Christ is promising them victory. Victory IN Him with a crown of life for each of them.

The church in Smyrna was made up of people who had truly sacrificed their lives, relationships and careers for the Lord Jesus Christ. They were the persecuted people, the persecuted church. In that region, to follow Christ meant you were not welcome in the "guilds," which were the ancient version of our modern "labor unions." If you could not be a part of a guild, you had no place to buy your raw goods, or sell your finished products.

The city of Smyrna is about 60 miles north of Ephesus and dates back over 2000 years before Christ. She was known as the "Port of Asia" because she had an excellent harbor for shipping to destinations all across the Aegean Sea. The church in this city struggled against two hostile forces: a Jewish population strongly opposed to Christianity, and a non-Jewish population that was loyal to Rome. Both worshiped the current Roman Emperor, who, he himself believed was a god. To be a Christian meant you did not worship the Emperor. Persecution and suffering where inevitable for those who chose to believe in the man known as Jesus Christ over the man-god, the current Emperor.

Let's take each verse and see what John was writing:

8 "And to the angel of the church in Smyrna write, 'These things says the First and the Last, who was dead, and came to life:"

The headquarters or gathering points of the guilds were on the agora which was the marketplace in the center of town. Built on a grand scale of beautiful marble columns, it also provided a walkway between the temples of the Greek gods: Zeus and Cybele. This agora was recognized as the most beautiful in the region. If you professed Jesus Christ, you could not be a member of a guild, which meant you could not work. That is why Jesus spoke to them saying "I know your afflictions and your poverty."

He knew that to choose Him would mean loss of income and possessions to the point of humiliation, demoralizing and complete poverty. Jesus knew as He was speaking to John; dictating this message to the church in Smyrna, that those who would follow Him and claim Him as their personal Lord and Savior would suffer greatly. But many did it anyway!

Temples to the gods Cybele and Dionysus (Greek) or Bacchus (Roman) were built here in Smyrna. These were important throughout the region which covered thousands of miles. People came from near and far to worship the pagan gods. Bacchus was the god of gluttony and everything in excess. The Bacchanalia which is a festival of orgies covered a two day span. Orgies of sexual immorality, food, drink and anything else were not only accepted, it was expected.

Ceremonies were performed in and around the temple of Cybele where it was considered an honor to mutilate ones-self and splatter their own blood on the stone altar. The more they self-mutilated and spilled their own blood, the more they felt they were honoring their pagan god.

Our Lord, Jesus shed His blood once for all. His blood was spilled at Calvary to cover all of our sins, each one of us. He is not a marble statue where birds will sit and visitors must travel to see. He is in our hearts; He is with us as we go about our daily lives. He is alive in us, an active part of who we are.

Q How is today's society similar-or different from this first century town? _____
_____
_____

Q Find at least 2 verses in the New Testament that refer to Jesus shedding His blood for you. _____
_____
_____

Q How do you feel about this sacrifice – the one He did just for YOU?_____
_____
_____
_____

9 "I know your works, tribulation, and poverty (but you are rich); and I know the blasphemy of those who say they are Jews and are not, but are a synagogue of Satan."

Jesus commended the church at Smyrna for its faith in suffering. He then encouraged the believers not to fear the future if they remain faithful. He said they will suffer, but not because of their sin.

He chastised the Jews who had joined forces with the pagan worshipers. These Jews were helping to persecute the Christians by making false statements about them. They were slandering the followers of Christ.

There was another group of people who followed the Jewish traditions, but they did not want to wear long hair or be circumcised as the Jews required. They did not like the new religion interfering with the way things were. They participated in all things Jewish, except the things they didn't like. This helped to create a pseudo-Jewish religion; one that did not honor the God of Abraham or the Lord Jesus Christ.

The term 'synagogue of Satan' is a term describing the Jewish house of worship: the synagogue. It was no longer a house of worship to the God of the Torah, to the God of Abraham, Isaac and Jacob. The pseudo-Jews and the Jewish population had joined forces with the pagans against the Christians. This is how they turned the house of worship into a synagogue of Satan. It meant that these

Jews were serving Satan's purposes not God's when they followed the evil plans of the pagans even as they gathered to worship.

Q In today's society, we find so many of the same challenges with which the first century church struggled. What areas of your life are your biggest struggles? _____
_____
_____
_____

Q I understand that Jesus knows these struggles, what can I do to separate myself from them?_____
_____
_____

10a *"Do not fear any of those things which you are about to suffer. Indeed, the devil is about to throw some of you into prison, that you may be tested, and you will have tribulation ten days."*

The term 10 days means that although persecution would be intense, it would be relatively short. It would have a definite beginning and a definite end and God would remain in complete control.

Jesus said the persecution would last ten days. We know that the Book of Revelation is a vision and the days rarely mean 24 hour periods. John returned to the mainland from the island of Patmos about 96-97 AD. In researching the history following this time period, there were 10 emperors who were against Christianity. They ruled this region for over three hundred years causing the church to suffer greatly. Finally in 313 AD Emperor Constantine signed into law an edict allowing Christians freedom to practice their faith. It was also decreed that all land and possessions must be returned to them. This ended the 10 "days" of persecution.

The ten emperors were: Nerva who died in 98, Trajan; 117, Marcus Aurelius; 180, Severus; 211, Maximinius; 238, Decius; 251, Valerian; 260, Aurelian; 275, Diocleation; 305 and Galerius; 311.

Q The reason we go through trials is to produce faith. Write about a trial you went through and how it increased your faith in God.
_____
_____
_____
_____

Q What would I tell someone who is going through a similar trial? How would I share Jesus in that situation?_____
_____
_____

10b *Be faithful until death, and I will give you the crown of life.*

God does not cause the persecution; He allows it to strengthen each of us as a testimony to our genuine faith in Him. Even though we go through trials and struggles, God has His hand over us; ready to stop Satan from reaching his ultimate goal of destroying us and our faith.

God allowed Satan to test this church in Smyrna. Satan's goal was to turn them from God or kill them. Jesus makes it clear that this church is faithful to prevent the death that Satan wanted them to have. That death is complete separation from God. Amazingly the church grew during this time! It appears the more it was persecuted, the more it grew.

Smyrna was famous for its athletic games. A crown of flowers or leaves was the trophy received by the champion at the conclusion of a sports event. Once more, Jesus knew that the faithful would understand there was a very special crown waiting for them.

They knew they were the true victors even in the most difficult of times. If we are faithful to Jesus Christ, we will receive the prize of victory: the crown and eternal life.

Have you ever heard of a victor's crown being placed on a person who has died? Of course not! A crown is recognition of importance. A person set apart: a high level of achievement. Doesn't this visual image help confirm the future of those who choose to follow Christ? Why would He promise us a crown of LIFE if we were not going to be able to wear it? Physical death is permanent. Our passing is simply moving from an earthly life to a heavenly life. We should not fear death, because as believers in Jesus Christ, it is simply change.

This message to the Smyrna Church was for them to remain faithful during their suffering because God is in control and his promises are reliable. Jesus never says that by being faithful to Him we will avoid troubles, suffering and persecution. Rather we must be faithful to Him during our sufferings. Only then will our faith prove to be genuine. We remain faithful by keeping our eyes on Christ and what He promises us now and in the future.

Believers and unbelievers alike experience physical death. All people will be resurrected, but believers will be resurrected to eternal life with God. Unbelievers will be resurrected to be punished with the second death, which is eternal separation from God.

Q This church grew in faith and numbers as it was persecuted. What do I do when I am under persecution? _____
_____
_____

Q What will my crown look like? The one I receive as I arrive in heaven. _____
_____
_____

Q What things must I do to keep my eyes on Christ? _____
_____
_____
_____

11 "He who has an ear, let him hear what the Spirit says to the churches. He who overcomes shall not be hurt by the second death."

Jesus wrote this letter to the church in Smyrna to provide comfort and encouragement. He knew the struggles they were going to endure, and He wanted them to know that He understood. This is a reminder that He had a reward waiting for them.

The first death referred to here is that of leaving our earthly life; our loved ones and our things. The second death, He mentions here, is what happens to us after we stand before Jesus Christ. Some people believe that will be upon our dying, others believe it will be at the end of the age. What we do know for sure is that scripture is clear when we breathe our last breath here on earth, at some point in God's perfect plan, <u>every knee will bow</u> before Jesus Christ. Not just His followers, not just those who did good works, but EVERY knee will bow.

Verse 11 says the church in Smyrna would be victorious and not hurt (suffer) anymore. What a beautiful thought for those early Christians who suffered so much! Let's read that verse again: *[11] "He who has an ear, let him hear what the Spirit says to the churches. He who overcomes shall not be hurt by the second death."*

Q How does this verse apply in my life today? I know Jesus knows what I am dealing with. But how does it help me? _____
_____
_____
_____

Q Is my faith strong enough to withstand tribulation and persecution from the world? Why/why not?_____
_____
_____
_____

Q A mark of a living church (or person) is their ability to withstand the pressures of the world. Lack of money, physical attacks, rumors, illnesses, gossip, etc.. Since I am a Temple, (or church,) for the Lord, what area(s) of my life do I still need to work on? _____
_____
_____
_____
_____
_____

Personal Notes

Menorahs carved into stone near the Synagogue

Archway and column of the Synagogue

Arches on the lower level of the Agora

Columns on the upper level of the Agora

PERGAMUM

The Compromising Church

Please read Revelation 2:12-17

After reading these verses, we realize that this is a great deal of information Jesus needed to convey to the church of Pergamum. When you realize what was going on in this city, it is a very short letter. It's only about 200 words!

Pergamum was a beautiful city nestled against the hills. A combined population of about 110,000, it was not a port city like Ephesus and Smyrna. Instead, she was the spiritual, cultural, medical and political center of Asia Minor. Let's look at each area...

Culturally: The library was a huge building which held over 200,000 scrolls and was recognized as the second largest library in the ancient world. People came from near and far to read the volumes. Most were scrolls.

A new way of capturing the written word had been developed into a format we are more familiar with; the book. Part of the reason for the change was that papyrus for scrolls was becoming more and more difficult to obtain, so parchment, which is made from young animal skins was created by the locals.

Another area of their cultured lives was theatrical. With a theater which held 10,000 people, productions, opera's and scholars' discussions were a regular part of their lives. Carved in a steep angle, high on the hill, the acoustics were perfect. A small stage was all that was needed to project the entertainment to every seat.

Medically: One of the gods; Asklepios, created a huge draw to the city of Pergamum. He was the Greek serpent god believed to have the powers of healing. His image was that of a bearded man holding a staff with a serpent wrapped around the shaft.

People came from all over the known world for healing, which created the need for building the first medical center. There was one catch for admission. The Doctors, who were really pagan priests would accept a person only if they felt the ailing person could be healed. If it was determined you were pregnant or terminal, you were not welcome. They did not want to be associated with death.

There was one more way to be accepted and healed quickly. Money! The amount they paid was in direct proportion to the number of days and the level of treatment they received. Upon their "healing," the person would leave the hospital and carve their name and the illness they no longer had on a marble pillar. Often the people who did not pay well were not asked to place their name on the pillars. The wealthy made the facility "look good."

The serpent was the focal point of this hospital. At the entrance, which was a long tunnel, the ailing person had to pass a white marble column which had a carving of a snake twisting around the pole. They were required to bow and worship it both on their way into the facility and after they were "healed" on their way out. More about that later.

Politically: Pergamum was considered to be the second Rome. Rome was where the Emperor lived: Pergamum was where the Emperor visited. Each Emperor could not resist the ego-stroking which happened here. In fact at the top of the acropolis there are five palaces. Each was for an Emperor. They could not even live in the previous Emperor's palace, they had to have a new one built a little higher on the hill. The region of Asia Minor looked to Pergamum for political answers, which is why it was good to worship the Emperor-god. Many believed that to get ahead, one must compromise. It is clear that politics helped to make-up the fabric of the town and giving in to what was politically correct would get you far.

The majority of the city was at the base of the acropolis. On the sides and top were the homes and palaces of the wealthy, and the temples to the pagan gods. There were at least 3 temples in which to worship the current Emperor. The goddess Athena also had her own temple of stately marble columns. Finally, the great altar to the Greek god: Zeus was the closest to the edge of the acropolis. Standing at the base of the acropolis, one could look up to the top and see the steps to the altar. Massive in size, including a 70 foot altar, it was used for pagan sacrifices.

The Greek god Asklepios was represented as the snake god. He had his territory on the edge of town, farthest from the acropolis. He was know as the healing god, taking the knowledge that a snake would shed it's skin and become new again. So man, believing in the god Asklepios, would receive new life by worshipping him. The logo used in modern medicine is that of two snakes wrapped around a center pole. I am not saying the pagan god is our modern medicine. Many, many men and women who bow their knee to Jesus Christ are called to be excellent physicians. I mentioned it to show how 2,000 years later, pagan gods and their symbols are still a part of our everyday life.

Q The acropolis was the highest point in town. It was where the major pagan temples were built. What "temples" have I built that are my highest priority? What "things" are more important than my relationship with Jesus? _____
_____
_____
_____

Q This church is known throughout history as the "Compromising Church." What do I do to compromise in my relationship with God and others? _____
_____
_____

Let's look at the verses one by one:

12 "And to the angel of the church in Pergamos write, 'These things says He who has the sharp two-edged sword:"

    The sharp, two-edged sword was something the people of that day understood. It was a warrior's fighting tool. In modern times, when we hear the term "assault rifle" we instantly know what it is and that its purpose is to kill. In the era John was writing to, a two-edged sword was instantly recognized as the ultimate tool to kill.

    The sword was used especially by infantrymen; the front line, the ones who were in the thick of the fighting. Often the owner engraved his name on the blade. The sword most popular with the Roman fighters was called a "gladius." It was forged from iron, about two feet long with both sides of the blade being equally sharp, the tip had a diamond point. Since it weighed about three pounds, it was easy to use, allowing the soldier to get close to his enemy and thrust the sword in any direction with deadly consequences.

The Lord is our two-edged sword. In *Hebrews 4:12 For the word of God is living and powerful, and sharper than any two-edged sword, piercing even to the division of soul and spirit, and of joints and marrow, and is a discerner of the thoughts and intents of the heart.* The word from God separates good from evil with no room for compromise.

Q The word of God is a two-edge sword. When has my word been like a two-edge sword? What were the results? _____
_____
_____

Q What should I have said?_____
_____
_____

13 "I know your works, and where you dwell, where Satan's throne is. And you hold fast to My name, and did not deny My faith even in the days in which Antipas was My faithful martyr, who was killed among you, where Satan dwells."

Jesus says He "knows where you dwell, where Satan has his throne." A throne is the chair – or most comfortable place - set apart for the head of the house: the lord of the home, or dwelling. Jesus knew that Satan felt very comfortable here in Pergamum. This was his home, he was comfortable here, and his throne was here.

Spiritually: there were four pagan gods who were worshipped here. The most important god, the one you wanted everyone to see you worshiping was the current Emperor. Each Emperor came into power so completely ego-centered that he believed himself to be a god. Of course his inner circle encouraged it because that brought them more fame and position. It was good to worship him on an outward and daily basis if you wanted any level of success. Your work and everything else about you was disregarded if you did not worship the Emperor.

There were three other major pagan gods who were worshipped here as well; each with their individual statues and temples. The Greeks worshiped more than one god at a time. They believed the more they worshiped, the better their chances for a good life. Greek gods and pagan worship; written about in enticing novels for our reading pleasure . . . the books many of us read today.

Next to the Emperor, Zeus was the largest god worshiped. His temple was magnificent. It met the needs of the lust of the eye, people were drawn to its striking marble beauty. Inside the massive structure was an altar. Sacrifices of humans and animals were performed regularly on this altar.

Jesus referred to His "faithful martyr Antipas" who lost his life here. The temple to Zeus was known for horrible crimes. During this period, men and women who professed Christ were placed inside a hollow, life-size brass bull. After locking them in, a fire was built under the bull causing the person inside to roast to death. It is not confirmed that this is how Antipas died. It is known as a horrible form of torture through recorded history of the time.

Jesus referred to this temple as the "Throne of Satan." An interesting side note. In 1930, a new museum of artifacts from Pergamum was completed and opened to the public. One of the main displays was purchased from Pergamum and transferred piece by piece to its new home in Berlin, Germany. The new display was the altar to

Zeus: The Throne of Satan, open for the general public to visit only three years before Hitler became chancellor of Germany.

The goddess Demetrius was the goddess of grain. She was worshipped for good harvests and plentiful food. Supposedly she forgave the sins of her followers if they submerged themselves in the blood of a bull; thus counterfeiting the Christian belief that we are washed in the blood of Jesus.

Dionysus was the son of the Greek god Zeus. Supposedly his mother was a human woman. This was the attempt by the pagans to appeal to Christians that Dionysus was no different than Jesus. A human mother and a god father. The belief was held that Dionysus turned water into wine at night in his temple. We know the pagans were trying to equal our Lord Jesus on this, His first miracle.

Satan was quite comfortable here. He had caused the Greeks and Romans to become fully depraved in their daily lives. To this day, in the Middle East, there is a saying: "if you must tell a lie to get what you want, it is acceptable."

Q Do I stay focused on God's word like the martyrs did? If not, Why not? _____
_____
_____

Q How am I like this church? _____
_____
_____

Q Jesus said He was pleased that the church *"hold fast to My name, and did not deny My faith."* How am I doing that today? _____
_____
_____

Q Do I get drawn into books I shouldn't be reading, or TV I shouldn't be watching? Why? _____
_____

14 "But I have a few things against you, because you have there those who hold the doctrine of Balaam, who taught Balak to put a stumbling block before the children of Israel, to eat things sacrificed to idols, and to commit sexual immorality."

Balak was the king of Moab mentioned in the Old Testament book of Numbers. He did not like seeing the multitudes of Israelites moving through the region, conquering the Amorites and others as they went. He feared for his own country.

King Balak called upon Balaam who some called a prophet; but in reality practiced "divination," or witchcraft, to help him discover what would happen with the Israelites. Would they conquer his country, or could he get enough information from this "prophet" to know how to fight them and retain his land?

Balaam was considered to be the best in his chosen profession. He even acknowledged that the God of the Israelites was a powerful god. Balaam would obey God's word and commands as long as it would profit him. By telling people they could eat the meat which had been sacrificed to the pagan gods and partaking in immoral relationships, he was using the same thought process as the serpent did in Genesis 3 when he twisted God's word leading Eve and Adam to fall.

He also promoted immoral sexual activity because he knew it was wrong and would cause people to fall into temptation. By encouraging infidelity and other sexual sins mentioned in the teachings of Jesus, he could keep the new believers in a compromising position with God. The church in Ephesus did not allow sexual sin. Yet the church here in Pergamum did allow it. Here we have compromise for political correctness.

Balaam presented a great option to those who did not have a close relationship with the One true God. He talked the talk, but did not give his heart. He led many people away by planting thoughts of compromise and deception.

Q Is it easy for me to compromise my actions? _____
_____

Q Maybe I need to ask myself WHY?_____
_____
_____

Q How do I compromise for political correctness when it is clear that Jesus taught against it? _____
_____
_____

Q When it involves a family member or loved one do I compromise?_____
_____

15 "Thus you also have those who hold the doctrine of the Nicolaitans, which thing I hate."

When Jesus says He hates something, it has to be important for us to take note and avoid. What and who were the Nicolaitans? The definition goes back to the great-grandson of Noah. His name was Nimrod. He did not follow in Noah's faith in God. He vowed to create a one world government controlled by religion and became a powerful tyrant who ruled over all of the known earth. He rebelled against God and insisted that the God of his fathers was not to be honored. At every opportunity Nimrod desecrated the laws of God, causing the faithful to weaken in their resolve, to avoid confrontation and finally rationalize their harden hearts.

Nimrod lived in modern Iraq and is considered to be the founder and creator of the Nicolaitans. He created a plan in order to unify the people into 'a one religious system' with the same beliefs, doctrines and trade program. It was meant to transform the lower class people into slaves, so that the Nicolaitans, who ran the system, could lead comfortable lives while making the slaves work.

When we take our eyes off of God and place them on someone else, whether it is religious, governmental, or even a pop cultural figure, we are not looking at our creator. We compromise God's position in our lives.

Q Do I associate with people who help me rationalize my wrong choices?_____ Why do I do that?_____
_____
_____
_____

Q What do I do that is not a problem for me, but might be a problem for someone I am with? Am I aware of others stumbling blocks? _____
_____
_____

16 "Repent, or else I will come to you quickly and will fight against them with the sword of My mouth."

Repent . . . *Webster*'s dictionary says it means "to feel or show that you are sorry for something bad or wrong that you did, and you want to do what is right." *The Free Dictionary* says: "2. To feel such regret for past conduct as to change one's mind regarding it: 3. To become a more moral or religious person as a result of remorse or contrition for one's sins."

If one did not make a conscience decision to feel true regret for their sin and return to the morals within the teachings of Jesus Christ, He, Jesus would "pierce" and "divide" their very being. This was how strongly He felt about the sin of compromise in Pergamum.

Q What area(s) of my life do I need to repent? _____
_____
_____

Q Why? _____
_____
_____

17 "He who has an ear, let him hear what the Spirit says to the churches. To him who overcomes I will give some of the hidden manna to eat. And I will give him a white stone, and on the stone a new name written which no one knows except him who receives it."

We have already learned about the white stone, the marble column on which people wrote their name and the condition from which they believed they had been healed as they left the hospital. It was The stone referred to here is the purest and whitest of stones. The white marble, pure white marble, is the most expensive stone of the day. In fact, it is still considered impossible to find a "pure" white stone. No blemishes, no markings, just milky white. Jesus is that "white stone" and our "heavenly" name, the name He calls us is written by Him into the book of Life. We will not need to write it or list our condition; it will simply be our name as only God can pronounce it. The faithful believers in this evil city were examples of His power in their lives. They were the stones God had washed clean in His blood.

Q How easy is it to slip into paganism, by reading the enticing stories, or watching videos. Sadly, today, many know more about the Greek gods than they do about the One True God. Where am I in my search for enticement and entertainment?
_____
_____

Q How does paganism look today? A few examples are the worship of sports figures, celebrities, materialism, etc. _____
_____
_____

Q Today, people reach out to God and do not get the reply they want. So, not trusting in God and His timing, they turn to card readers, horoscopes, Oiji boards, and other forms of pagan worship. This is compromise of God's word. In what ways do I compromise my faith? _____
_____
_____

Q Am I comfortable allowing those who choose to live biblically immoral lives to be in leadership in my church? _____
_____
My community? _____
_____

Q What action can I take to change it? _____
_____
_____

Road leading to acropolis. Temples are on the top. The theater is near the top facing this way.

Temple ruins on top of the Acropolis.

Stone column with snakes honoring the god Asklepios.

Stones in foreground have names of people "healed" by Asklepios

Thyatira

The Corrupt Church

Please read Revelation 2: 18-29

The fourth stop on the Roman Road is Thyatira, sitting about 30 miles southeast of Pergamum. We have now turned further inland, away from the Aegean Sea. The climate changes and we lose the challenges that come from cities who gain their income from the oceans. However, it is clear there are many issues here. As we learn about the seven churches, we discover that Thyatira was the least important from a worldly perspective. However, this letter, which Jesus dictated to John, is the longest! Does it mean that they had the biggest problems? No, it means He needed to make clear to His followers what the problems were.

We have learned that each church we have visited so far was special in its own right. It was doing things "good," and in most of them, it was doing things that were "wrong."

The word Thyatira means "the citadel or castle of Thya." It had been a fortified military outpost before it became a thriving town. As far back as 282 B.C., it was part of the state of Pergamum. Just as we live in our city, which is in our state, Thyatira was the city under the rule of Pergamum. It was the first line of defense as the Syrian and Pergamum armies battled back and forth.

The value of this town for generations was a front line for the defending rulers. They were the first to get shot at, the first to see the enemy. Their responsibility was to cause disarray and slow the speed of the advancing enemy.

As Roman rule finally took over, around 190 B.C., Thyatira developed and advanced. Archaeologists have found coins from that time period which indicate they were developing a commercial existence before the first century.

Inscriptions found on the coins mention workers in wool, linen, leather, bronze, and pottery. There were tanners and bakers as well. One of the main industries was the dying of fabric – mainly the colors of crimson and purple. This included Lydia, mentioned in Acts 16:14 *"Now a certain woman named Lydia heard us. She was a seller of purple from the city of Thyatira, who worshiped God. The Lord opened her heart to heed the things spoken by Paul."*

Once more we find that each industry had a "guild:" a union, or association which the workers must belong to in order to buy or sell goods. If you professed to be a follower of Jesus Christ, you would lose your right to be part of the guild and thus lose your source of income and your ability to buy raw materials and sell the finished product. Plus, one would loose their position in the community.

This was a "corrupt church." The church of Thyatira had betrayed Jesus and all that He represented. They had returned to their lover; the love of pagan worship. Many who had not committed their hearts to Jesus had fallen for the lies and delusions being taught by the pagan world.

Q This town was a "front line" for warring parties, yet they did not fight for Jesus. When do I find myself not fighting for Him?___

_____
_____

Q There are times in my life where I find myself wanting to blend in and be politically correct. Why is that not acceptable to Jesus? _____

---

18 "And to the angel of the church in Thyatira write, These things says the Son of God, who has eyes like a flame of fire, and His feet like fine brass:

The term "son of God" is a title of Jesus. It is only used in the letter to this church and is not found anywhere else in the book of Revelation. In the Greek religion, Zeus was the supreme god. He had a son named Apollo who was supposedly born from an earth mother. The Greeks were able to use this god to corrupt WHO Jesus was, by saying He was just another son of a god, born to an earthly woman.

By announcing that Jesus was "the son of God," in the letter to this church, He was reminding them of His divine position, His unique authority, which was far superior to that of the pagan gods and cult religions they lived and worked among. He was not one of the sons; He was THE son of The God.

The people of Thyatira worked with their hands. They understood the "flame of fire" for creating tools of war and peace. The potter knew the flame of fire for finishing his craft. The people who dyed fabric needed the flame of fire to seal in their colors. There was understanding in the term "the flame of fire." It held power, yet it could also destroy.

Jesus referred to "fine brass" in this scripture. Once more, He was speaking in terms the people could understand. One of the major industries was the creation of items made in bronze. The Bronze Guild was bigger than all of the guilds in Thyatira. Burnished or fine bronze was the "finished" product.

Q What I have read so far about this church, I see that today's world has similar issues. Am I a part of the issues, or am I helping others to draw closer to Christ? How?_____
_____
_____

Q How is Jesus different than the sons of Zeus? _____
_____
_____

Q What did He do that the pagan gods could not do?_____
_____
_____

19 *"I know your works, love, service, faith, and your patience; and as for your works, the last are more than the first."*

The faithful of this church were good, hard workers. They went above and beyond to walk the Christian walk, to love as Christ taught; which was the evidence of their true faith: their deeds.

Yet many who claimed to follow Christ had not truly accepted the faith, replacing it with rituals and pagan celebrations. Pagan temples were converted into Christian temples, religious festivals and various symbols of the pagan worship were re-branded as Christian. They had found a way to corrupt their faith and be complacent in their walk with God: a way to make it look good, while doing what they wanted.

In John 15:18-19 we read about the world's hatred of Christ as He talks to the people in Israel. *18 If the world hates you, you know that it hated Me before it hated you. 19 If you were of the world, the world would love its own. Yet because you are not of the world, but I chose you out of the world, therefore the world hates you.*

As believers in Jesus Christ, we are to guard our hearts and minds; to be aware of wrong suggestions and ideas that slip into our own thoughts and those of the church. If Jesus would not accept it, we shouldn't either.

Q   Many churches teach that God will not judge me based on my works. He will only judge me based on my faith. This verse clearly states that He is aware of my works and my faith. How do I show my faith THROUGH my works? _____

Q   How can I show my faith through my love, service and patience? _____

Q   As a person walking by faith, how am I guarding my heart from the corruption all around me? _____

Q   Do I have family and friends whose hearts I need to be praying for? List their names._____

20 Nevertheless I have a few things against you, because you allow that woman Jezebel, who calls herself a prophetess, to teach and seduce My servants to commit sexual immorality and eat things sacrificed to idols.

Jezebel's father was a priest to a pagan god. She grew up in this belief and had become a devout member of that cult, in her mind; a prophetess. She used every opportunity to spread the pagan religion of Baal as completely as she could throughout the region.

She was the wife of the Jewish King: Ahab, who ruled over northern Israel for over 60 years around 870 B.C. She was the epitome of evil and her husband was the epitome of lack-of-leadership. She convinced him to build an altar to the pagan god Baal and to worship there. He left his Jewish faith to please her.

Saying her name conjures up her legacy of witchcraft, revenge, manipulation, immorality and cruelty. She was a woman who truly wanted to destroy God, to the point that she ordered the murder of Godly prophets. Today, almost 3,000 years after her death, her name still represents the essence of wickedness and the power of seduction which many still use.

Immorality was and is a sin. People tend to categorize or quantify sin. Was it a big or little sin? Sin is sin. No sin is acceptable to God. NONE. Sexual sin is no different. In the letter to Thyatira, Jesus reminds them that the sin of immorality leads people away from Him.

The eating of food which had been sacrificed to pagan gods was a major issue with the new converts. As Jews, they had strict guidelines in how to prepare an animal for an offering or sacrifice. God required His people to drain the blood before presenting it to Him at the altar. Pagans did not care; they sacrificed the animal with blood still in the body.

The meat that was offered for sale in the marketplace was left over from the sacrifice to false gods. For a person practicing their Jewish faith and traditions, this meat was part of idol worship, sacrificed with the blood still in it, and therefore not to be eaten. At the time she was alive, Jezebel, the Queen and pagan goddess, encouraged the people to eat the meat from those sacrifices. Hundreds of years later, the tradition of eating sacrificed animals in the pagan religion was still strongly encouraged. Many of the new followers of Christ were from the Jewish background and struggled with those traditions and new teachings. This caused great conflict and confusion on the part of the new believers in Jesus.

Q Sin is something we all struggle against. Do I allow sexual sin to enter my life through the books I read, or the movies I watch?
_____
_____

Q Does my loving Lord like to see and hear what I say and do all of the time?_____
_____

Q Do I think it is okay to take Him to see violent or sexually graphic "entertainment?"_____
_____

Q Why do I like that kind of "entertainment?"_____
_____
_____

Q I may not eat things sacrificed to idols, but do I eat things that are unhealthy for me -"a temple of God?"_____
_____
_____

21 "And I gave her time to repent of her sexual immorality, and she did not repent."

To repent, one must change direction and seek forgiveness from the person who was offended and change personal behavior. They must make a concise decision to improve and not repeat the past sin.

In the eyes of the pagans, they were doing nothing wrong. They saw nothing to ask forgiveness from, and no need to be forgiven. Their hearts were hardened to the teachings of Christ. They liked their sin and saw no need to change.

Jesus is rebuking His people in this letter; reminding them that He will not allow sin to infiltrate His church. He sees that they have allowed the spirit of Jezebel into their lives. They tolerate, in fact they embrace her and her teachings. This is total corruption of their faith.

Sexual sin in modern times can range from what one watches on TV, online or reads. This includes the so-called 'romance' stories you would not share with Christ if He were sitting on your couch, next to you. It also includes what you do with someone other than your husband or wife that is not acceptable in a Bible based marriage.

Q   Jesus said that He gave the church time to repent of their sexual immorality. Since I know what He expects, how much longer do I think He will give me?_____
_____

Q   Have I rationalized my choices to the point of "corruption?"____
_____
_____

22 "Indeed I will cast her into a sickbed, and those who commit adultery with her into great tribulation, unless they repent of their deeds."

The bed of suffering is believed to be the time of great tribulation. A time where those who have chosen to live their lives without Christ will have no protection from evil.

The priests who ministered to the pagan goddess's were considered neither male nor female. They assumed their positions as males. After confirming their true desire to become a pagan priest, one would complete his dedication by drinking a potion containing opium. They would then self castrate. Thus they would have no sexual desires and became focused completely on their goddess.

In the temples, there were also male and female prostitutes who did not care if the adulterous encounter was with their same gender or the opposite. Homosexuality was widespread in pagan worship, encouraged by the Jezebel spirit.

Those who were committing adultery were not only participating in the act of sexual sin, they were also participating in an adulterous relationship with the pagan gods. Many tried to justify their compromise, but Jesus is making it very clear that unless they repent of their ways, they will "suffer intensely."

If we look at the following scripture, I think it is pretty clear what Jesus is saying to the people in Thyatira. *Matthew 7: 21-23 21 "Not everyone who says to Me, 'Lord, Lord,' shall enter the kingdom of heaven, but he who does the will of My Father in heaven. 22 Many will say to Me in that day, 'Lord, Lord, have we not prophesied in Your name, cast out demons in Your name, and done many wonders in Your name?' 23 And then I will declare to them, 'I never knew you; depart from Me, you who practice lawlessness!'*

Jesus wanted them to have a clear picture of where He stands on adultery and all other sins of compromise. When we say we are believers and then do not follow His teachings and corruption, He will have nothing to do with us on judgment day.

Q   How am I justifying the Jezebel spirit in my life? _____
_____

Q   If I <u>don't</u> agree with this message to the church of Thyatira, who am I rejecting? _____

Q   If I <u>do</u> agree with this letter, who am I rejecting? _____

Q   How will my eternal life be if I continue rejecting the teachings of Jesus? _____

23 "I will kill her children with death, and all the churches shall know that I am He who searches the minds and hearts. And I will give to each one of you according to your works."

The children are the followers of Jezebel. They have chosen pagan worship, both directly and indirectly, over walking the narrow path of Christ. Jesus said from the time He started His ministry that he wants your heart. If He has your heart, He will have your mind. When He has your mind, He can provide peace, wisdom and understanding. His promise here is to bless each of us based on our commitment to Him, which is evident by our "works." When we love Him, we want to serve Him and others.

Q   What do you think Jesus meant when He said He "will kill her children with death?" _____

EXPLORING THE SEVEN CHURCHES OF REVELATION

Q How will it be different for "her children" than it will be for those who follow Jesus' teachings? _____

Q When He is searching my mind and my heart, what will He find? _____

Q Since He is going to give to each of us according to our works, what am I doing, and what more could I be doing to increase my "works?" _____

24 "Now to you I say, and to the rest in Thyatira, as many as do not have this doctrine, who have not known the depths of Satan, as they say, I will put on you no other burden."

In speaking to the "rest" of the followers, the ones who were walking as Christ's followers, Jesus encouraged them to avoid the teachings of Jezebel. In pagan worship there are secrets. Study any organization in your daily life and see if it is open and welcoming to everyone. If there are secret meetings or secret messages, they are not and can not be of a Godly nature. But let me stress this point. If you or someone you know is involved in an organization that holds secret meetings, no amount of justification will replace God's word. No rationalizing or compromise will cover the fact you are doing something in the dark and you will not be blessed.

God's world is open. Open for all to see. Satan's world is full of deep secrets including the traditions and false teachings of pagan worship. It tempts people to participate, to think they are special or set apart. Sadly, that "separation," that "specialness" is separation from God, not man. He says here in verse 24 that He will not put any other burden on those who hold to His teachings. No secrets to keep, no dark places in which to hide.

Q It appears He is speaking directly to me and the faithful in Thyatira. What doctrine is He referring to in this verse? _____
_____
_____

Q How can I avoid this doctrine? _____
_____
_____

Q I have not known the depths of Satan, so I know that He will not put on me any more burdens. What does that mean to me? ____
_____
_____

25 *"But hold fast what you have till I come."*

Read that again. "But hold fast what you have till I come." How simple, yet how difficult. Jesus is encouraging the faithful of Thyatira to stay focused on Him.

Q What can I do to "hold fast" to Him? _____
_____
_____

26 *"And he who overcomes, and keeps My works until the end, to him I will give power over the nations-"*

The end that Jesus mentions here is the end of the age. He is giving His word to those who choose to stand faithful. They will stand with Him as He judges the nations.

Q Specifically, how do I keep His works until the end? _____
_____
_____

Q   Why do I want to have "power over the nations?" _____
_____
_____
_____

27 "He shall rule them with a rod of iron; They shall be dashed to pieces like the potter's vessels'- as I also have received from My Father;"

When Jesus walked this earth, much of the time He spoke to the people in parables. Those were stories people could understand. For the people of this church, he spoke about iron and pottery because they were craftsmen. They worked with their hands with iron and clay. They understood how grand an iron scepter was. How strong and unbreakable it could be in a warrior's hand. It was stronger and more expensive than bronze. The blade could be sharpened to slice bone as if it were butter.

The potter knew broken pottery. He knew that a broken pot was damaged goods, not usable, a waste. One must start over when the pot would break. The One in leadership - the One who would rule throughout the ages: He would judge those who chose to be the "broken pottery," the worshippers of pagan gods instead of Jesus Christ.

The faithful ones will have the protection and the security of the iron scepter. They will not be dashed to pieces. Those who do not give their hearts to Him will feel that separation. This pledge IS upheld by the authority given to Jesus from God the Father.

Q   Write this verse in modern language so that believers and unbelievers will understand. _____
_____
_____

28 "and I will give him the morning star."

Step outside in the early morning and look to the heavens, a morning star appears just before dawn. This is the coldest and darkest time of night; right before the sun rises. The earth is at its lowest or darkest point. Christ is saying to the true believers in Thyatira that He is their morning star. He is preparing to burst upon the scene, exposing evil with his light of truth and bringing his promised reward. He is giving hope.

Q We stand on that hope, as well. It is not a "I sure hope it happens," kind of hope. What has Jesus taught me that gives me that 100% "hope" in Him? _____
_____

Q Where in scripture can I find this proof? _____
_____

Q How do I glorify Him on a daily basis? (Hint: 2 Chronicles 7:14)
_____
_____

29 "He who has an ear, let him hear what the Spirit says to the churches."

Jesus is reminding the faithful to trust what they are hearing. Since many people in that day could not read, the letter would have been read out loud. The Spirit is telling them the truth. Since the church was filled with those who were not living for Christ, He wanted them to hear it from Him. This was His seal, His mark on the letter, giving credibility.

Q As we complete the letter to the church in Thyatira, what do I hear from the Spirit? _____
_____

Bales of cotton on their way to the processing center

Column base and upper arch from an entryway

Ruins of a temple

A sarcophagus in the foreground, various columns and arches are all that remain.

SARDIS
The Dead Church

Please read Revelation 3:1-6

We continue along the Roman road traveling about one and a half hours southeast of Thyatira. Sardis was on the main road leading from the sea to the interior of the empire, creating a cultural and wealthy lifestyle. This was the crossroads of goods, ideas, customs, knowledge and beliefs.

Sardis had a reputation that it lived, but was dead. Today, one can view the well-preserved and partly restored ruins of this once magnificent city. It contains a large Temple to the goddess Artemis, which was known as one of the largest in the area. A sports arena which sat thousands, a multi storied gymnasium, huge public bath houses and a theatre which also sat thousands.

The surrounding foothills and valleys were rich in fertile land due to several tributaries of the river Pactolus, which provided water and rich soil for the people of Sardis. Forests cover the rolling mountainous terrain where caves with veins of gold still exist. In the first century gold was removed from these caves and used for many things. Most importantly, it was used to make jewelry. Precious and semi-precious stones where bought and sold and used in the creation of beautiful pieces of jewelry. Artisans honed their crafts in this wealthy town and were known throughout the empire for creating fine quality jewels and craftsmanship.

The gold was also spun into thin, fine thread and used in making fabric for clothing. Both men and women wore this beautiful fabric. The more gold one wore in an outfit would signify the higher one's stature or position in the community.

The original town was built around 500 B.C. on a plateau; an acropolis, high above the surrounding plains. Because of the steep cliffs on the sides of the acropolis, the people of Sardis were confident the city was impregnable. Often there were no guards on duty watching for potential enemies. This, sadly, was their downfall. The townspeople went about their daily lives; the enemy could climb the cliffs, usually at night in areas not guarded. Capture and defeat came quickly.

On top of the acropolis, or upper town, the wealthy citizens and royalty lived in their palaces and mansions. At the base, a stream ran past the fortified - unprotected - acropolis. Throughout recorded history, this stream has been famous for rich deposits of gold, believed to have washed down from the caves above.

Near the water's edge there is a newer town. Built by the Romans, it was home to the working class. During the period of time at or near the beginning of the first century A.D., a huge building was constructed in the lower town which contained a gymnasium and bath. It was built in the typical grand proportions of the Roman Empire on prime real estate. Used by both the average and wealthy, it was a gathering place for all.

In 17 AD, there was a major earthquake which destroyed much of the region. It was reported by Roman and Greek historians. At least 12 cities in the surrounding area were completely destroyed. The quake came during the night. It was so sever that Rome sent aid packages to Sardis to help rebuild. The

Emperor also decreed that no taxes were to be paid to Rome for five years to allow funding for re-building.

As a side note: several centuries later a Jewish synagogue was built in the gymnasium complex. Scratched into one of the walls is the Greek word "tolerance." Why did the Greeks write this on a wall in a Jewish synagogue?

Q It is hard to imagine that people would have so much going for them, yet were not proactive in protecting it. Yet, as we look at our world, our country, our state and our town, aren't we suffering from similar issues? Lord, reveal to me what areas of my life are dead to You. _____
_____
_____

Q What can I do to change those dead areas? _____
_____
_____

1 "And to the angel of the church in Sardis write, 'These things says He who has the seven Spirits of God and the seven stars: "I know your works, that you have a name that you are alive, but you are dead.

Jesus is speaking; He has completed our salvation by dying, and rising from that death. He says that these are His words; He holds the seven spirits of God and the seven stars. Seven is God's perfect number. It is the sign of completion, which He is.

The reputation of Sardis was that of being an "alive" city. Considering their position of commerce on a major trade route, one would see them as being very much alive. Yet, they were dead in their faith. In Sardis there was a temple to the pagan goddess Artemis. It was so beautiful and grand that it became known as one of the most beautiful in the Ancient World. To a non-believer in Jesus, the question would be simply put: Why would a person choose to worship a God they could not see when they could be a follower of a goddess with such a grand temple? Purchasing icons which represented the goddess would provide a physical item one could see and touch and even talk to. While choosing to follow Jesus would mean being faithful to a non-touchable God.

When a person says they are a baker, you know they bake. When someone says they are a wood carver, you know they carve wood. When a Christian professes Jesus, they are taking on the position of being alive in Christ. If he or she is living a life that does not honor Christ, but say they are a Christian, they are living a lie. They are dead to Him. And He knows that person's heart!

Q Would people who don't know me well be surprised to find out I am a Christian? _____
_____
_____

Q Does that make me appear alive, or dead in Christ?_____
_____
_____

Q Why? What am I doing, or not doing to receive that opinion___
_____
_____

2 "Be watchful, and strengthen the things which remain, that are ready to die, for I have not found your works perfect before God."

This is a dramatic warning to the church of Sardis. They

were playing at being followers of Christ. They were not complete in His sight. The early church had been a very active church, as all of the others had been. Now, they were busy doing "things." Their deeds consisted of making it look good. Not reaching the hearts of those who worshipped the pagan gods.

Q What was missing in their relationship with Jesus? _____
_____
_____

Q What is missing in <u>my</u> relationship with Jesus? _____
_____
_____

3 "Remember therefore how you have received and heard; hold fast and repent. Therefore if you will not watch, I will come upon you as a thief, and you will not know what hour I will come upon you."

Many of the people did not read, so this letter would have been read out loud to the entire church. Jesus wants them to remember this important letter. To remember how they received it and heard it. Only then would they repent and turn back to Him.

This letter was something the people of Sardis could understand. The enemy conquered them on numerous occasions when they were not watching, when they were not on guard and mainly at night.

Even the earthquake of 17 AD came at night, when they were not expecting it. They could understand the concept that Jesus used here as a thief coming, because they knew the history of their town and how things happened when least expecting them.

They would not know when He would come, but they understood that He would come in His timing and they needed to be watching.

Q   What is He telling me to "hold fast" to? _____
_____
_____

Q   What do I need to do (right now) to be ready for His untimed return? _____
_____
_____

4 You have a few names even in Sardis who have not defiled their garments; and they shall walk with Me in white, for they are worthy.

In Sardis and throughout the Lydian region clothing of a gold color was very popular. To be told they would walk with Jesus dressed in white was setting them apart. Telling them they would be different. He knew they would not want to look and dress like the others if they were His followers. He wanted them in His purity, His color of white. And why did He say this? Because they were worthy!

The truly faithful followers of Jesus had not "soiled their clothes." They had not given in to temptations, greed or compromise. They had not crossed the line with paganism, sexual immorality or improper life choices. Social and cultural standards in Roman and Asian society were both tempting and intoxicating, Jesus is encouraging the faithful to stay true to their beliefs; to not soil their garments.

The color "white" in biblical terms equates to purity. How rewarding this must have been for those who were truly following

Him. What peace to know they would be clothed in white and walk with Jesus Christ, Himself. What a goal to focus on... even for us!

Q Would Jesus say that my name was one of those who had not defiled my garments? _____
_____
_____

Q After reading Mark 9:2-3, why is the term "clothed in white" so important for me to understand? _____
_____
_____
_____
_____

Q When I get to walk with Jesus in His "white," what does this scripture say about me? _____
_____
_____
_____

5 "He who overcomes shall be clothed in white garments, and I will not blot out his name from the Book of Life; but I will confess his name before My Father and before His angels."

When Jesus repeats Himself, He really wants us to understand what He is saying. The fact that He mentions being dressed in white in two verses, tells us how important this is to Him. Jesus is confirming that those who choose to make a change in their lives to "overcome" will be dressed in white.

He is the "white" they will be dressed in, and He will place their names in the book of life. Can you imagine Jesus sitting down at the right hand of His father and pointing at you He, says something like "Dad, see that one? That one is one of ours." As He is saying that, the angles begin to sing!

For those residents of Sardis who were trying to decide if they wanted to accept Christ, this could surly make a strong statement for them to do so. Imagine, Christ talking to his Dad about you.

Q This verse says that "he who overcomes." What do I need to do so that I can overcome and how do I do it? _____
_____
_____

Q Why is the Book of Life an important place to have my name?
_____
_____

6 "He who has an ear, let him hear what the Spirit says to the churches."

This is His reminder that He is speaking to each one of them. Most of the people did not read, so "he who has an ear" was a suggestion that it was time to listen! He lovingly wants them to come alive again and stand firm in their faith.

Q Lord, am I listening to You? Am I really listening to the things You want me to know? This is what I am hearing from You right now. .
_____
_____
_____
_____
_____
_____
_____
_____

Columns at the Temple of Artemis – Susan is standing at the base of the last one on the right.

Inner section of the gymnasium.
David is walking towards us, he is over 6' tall

Part of the fortification on the top of the acropolis

Susan is standing among the columns of the Temple to Artemis with the Acropolis in the background

PHILADELPHIA
The Faithful Church

Please read Revelation 3:7-13

Founded in 189 B.C., Philadelphia received its name from King Eumenes in honor of the love he had for his brother Attalus. In 17 A.D. the same earthquake that destroyed so much of the surrounding area nearly destroyed this city as well. The people were able to rebuild using their own money because Emperor Tiberius canceled the taxation imposed by Rome for five years.

Philadelphia sits near the Cogmus River and is about 35 miles from Sardis. Volcanic cliffs rise near the city allowing the ground to be very fertile and excellent for growing grapes. The wine from this area was of such great quality that it sold throughout the entire Roman Empire.

Along with the wine came the worship of Dionysus, the Greek god of fertility and wine. Since there has been very little excavation of this area, we must rely on the written historical record for this church. Along with the pagan temples to false gods came the sin. Sexual immorality, compromise and temptation are just a few of the issues the faithful dealt with on a daily basis.

Industry in this area included agriculture. Wine and olive oil were the two main crops. These were the only industries that Rome taxed. The government knew the items were manufactured in large quantities, so there would be more dollars to tax.

Hand crafted jewelry and perfume were also made here in Philadelphia. Because they were created as smaller items, Rome had no way of knowing the number of completed products created so they did not tax them.

The letters to the churches in Philadelphia and Smyrna were the only two which did not receive any form of condemnation. Because they were so very faithful, Jesus spoke to them through these letters in words of encouragement and uplifting support. He said he will protect them through upcoming trials and they trusted Him.

It is clear that this congregation was faithful to His teachings. They were a persecuted group, but did not respond to the attacks of the pagan community in a un-Christ like way.

These first century Christians, did not have an easy life. Most of them had come from a Jewish background. Knowing in their heart that Jesus was the true Messiah, they converted, yet their upbringing and their neighbors told them this was wrong. Persecution was a way of life for this young church. The division between the Jews and the Christians came down to the fundamental understanding of *who* Jesus was. Both religions felt *they* were God's chosen people.

As we look at the individual verses, we get a clearer picture of this important message from Jesus:

7 *"And to the angel of the church in Philadelphia write, 'These things says He who is holy, He who is true, "He who has the key of David, He who opens and no one shuts, and shuts and no one opens"*

Jesus is making it clear that He is the One. He is Holy and He is True. There is no question as to Who He is referring to in this statement. It is very important that the faithful in Philadelphia understood they were following the correct saviour. Earlier in the introduction to Revelation, we discussed how Jesus identified Himself. He said in *Revelation 1: 18* *"I am He who lives, and was dead, and behold, I am alive forevermore. Amen. And I have the keys of Hades and of Death."*

The second part of this verse is so exciting! "The key of David" what is the key of David? Mentioned in Isaiah 22:22; the Lord says: *"The key of the house of David I will lay on his shoulder; So he shall open, and no one shall shut; And he shall shut, and no one shall open."* Again it is the same wording as we just read in Revelation, chapter 1 and in chapter 3. It is clear to the author of Isaiah that the holder of the "key" is God.

In ancient times, the key was a sign of position, power, control or wealth, often worn by the women as a piece of jewelry. When a man was given a key, it was placed on the left shoulder, similar to the modern epaulette, or shoulder bars, worn by military officers, showing their rank, or authority.

We read in Acts 13: 22 David was called "a man after God's own Heart." David was many things, but the one thing he was always known for was his worship of the Lord. He danced, sang, lay prostrate and worshipped Him all the days of his life. That is David's key to God's heart. Let me repeat that. Remaining in constant worship is the key to God's heart. David had that key. When your heart is truly unlocked by God, it can not be shut by man. God is also the One who can shut the door of hell for us, which no one can open.

I believe the people in Philadelphia understood the "key." We know Jesus always spoke in words and phrases the people would understand and He knew this church was a faithful church.

Q Do I need to have the "key of David?" _____
_____

Q What do I need to do to have that key?_____
_____
_____

Q Can anyone get it for me?_____ Why/why not? _____
_____
_____

8 "I know your works. See, I have set before you an open door, and no one can shut it; for you have a little strength, have kept My word, and have not denied My name."

Jesus is encouraging them. The city was centrally located on the main Roman postal highway which allowed the local church to share the Gospel to those travelling through town, or merchants who had come to purchase goods. They also were open to much condemnation from those same travellers.

Jesus simply states that He knows their struggles. He reminds them that He has opened heaven to them because they have been faithful in keeping His word.

The Jews in this city did not keep their own ancient laws. It interfered in their sinful lusts. They also disrespected and degraded the Christians. Jesus knew the faithful converts wanted to see Him face to face, but were struggling so much against the sin around them. They were so tired!

Q Once more Jesus talks about their works. Read James 2:14-17. What does this mean to you in relationship to Revelation 3:8?
_____
_____

Q How does my life compare with this church? _____
_____
_____

9 "Indeed I will make those of the synagogue of Satan, who say they are Jews and are not, but lie - indeed I will make them come and worship before your feet, and to know that I have loved you."

In the churches we have already studied, the "synagogue of Satan" was a Jewish temple that defiles the Jews and their religion. There has been no archaeological evidence of the Jews in Philadelphia. We do know that stones which have Menorahs carved into them have been excavated several miles from the town. However, based on historical writings and the information in this letter we must believe there was an active community.

According to historical writings, the Jews in this area claimed that the kingdom belongs to the Jewish community, but Jesus is making it clear that they lie. At the end of the age, the statement of Philippians 2:10-11 will be fulfilled. Paul says: *10 that at the name of Jesus every knee should bow, of those in heaven, and of those on earth, and of those under the earth, 11 and that every tongue should confess that Jesus Christ is Lord, to the glory of God the Father.*

Quite clearly Jesus is reminding the faithful that they will be with Him, as the ungodly are forced to bow before them.

Q Describe how it will look as I stand with Jesus and watch the un-Godly come and worship at His feet. _____
_____
_____

Q Why would they worship at my feet? What have I done to be worthy?_____
_____

10 *"Because you have kept My command to persevere, I also will keep you from the hour of trial which shall come upon the whole world, to test those who dwell on the earth."*

What an encouragement! To know that Jesus has just promised them that because they have kept His command to persevere, to hang in there and not give up, or give in, He will keep them from tribulation.

Q What is going on in my life that I need this verse? What do I need to have to persevere, or keep going" _____
_____
_____

Q What is meant by the "hour of trial" in this verse? _____
_____
_____

11 *"Behold, I am coming quickly! Hold fast what you have, that no one may take your crown."*

"Hold fast what you have." What they have is Him! Their salvation, His love, the victor's crown! They have won the race and He is making sure they understand they will receive that special recognition: the crown. Everything that a Christian hopes for, they have. Hold fast!

Q What do I need to do to "hold fast?" _____
_____
_____

12 He who overcomes, I will make him a pillar in the temple of My God, and he shall go out no more. I will write on him the name of My God and the name of the city of My God, the New Jerusalem, which comes down out of heaven from My God. And I will write on him My new name.

In constructing a large building, an important part would be the pillars which provide support, durability and strength: the pieces that hold everything in place. Jesus is promising this church, because they overcome; they will be "pillars" in His temple.

Throughout the Old Testament we read passages where a stone was placed in a certain spot and dedicated to God. Often the stones were called "alters" or "pillars." This was a special recognition of The Holy One. To this day in the deserts of the Middle East it is possible to find these "pillars." Over 145 sites have been documented as ancient sacred stones. The people in Philadelphia understand from their ancestors what a "pillar" meant to God, and therefore understood what Jesus was saying in this letter to them.

An interesting side note: as we visited modern day Philadelphia there were three pillars which have been excavated from a church built several hundred years after this letter was written. All that remains of the massive structure are three pillars!

The city of Philadelphia was also familiar with name changes. The nickname in ancient times was 'Little Athens,' due to the many pagan temples which produced sin in so many forms. Its original name was Philadelphia, then it became Decapolis, then Neo-Kaisaria, then Flavia and is now called Ala-shehir, yet it is still referred to as Philadelphia. So receiving a new name, this time, the name of the Lord and God they worshipped, was exciting and encouraging for their faithfulness.

Let's take it to another level. Jesus said He will make them a pillar, He will write on them God's name and the city of God, AND, He will write on them God's new name! Count that! Three times in one verse He claims them in writing!

Q Where do I fit in? Am I an over comer? _____
_____

Q The struggles that I have are no better or worse than those of the people in Philadelphia. Write out exactly what Jesus said He will do for me. _____
_____
_____

Q How does that make me feel? _____
_____

13 *"He who has an ear, let him hear what the Spirit says to the churches."*

We know the faithful did hear this message because it was read out loud and they wanted so much to serve Him.

Q What is going on in my life that is keeping me from hearing what the Spirit is saying? _____
_____
_____

Very little excavation has been done here, only a few columns and stone building foundations.

Excavation of structures surrounding the ancient church

One of three pillars from a church built several hundred years after the letter to the Church in Philadelphia.

Two pillars and a modern Muslim minaret in the distance.

LAODICEA

The Lukewarm Church

Please read Revelation 3:14-22

Laodicea is located in the Lycus Valle in the region of Phrygia. It was founded around 260 B.C. by Antiochus II Theos, king of Syria. The original name was Diospolis which meant "City of Zeus." The king renamed the city in honor of his wife, Laodice. Originally built as a fortification from warring parties, it became the first line of defense for the King's territory.

Today, to travel by car from Philadelphia to Laodicea, would take about one hour. The Lycus River flows a few miles in the distance, which provided some of the water to this town. In the opposite direction are hot mineral springs which sit half way up the mountain, about 8 miles away. The hot water from these springs was also piped to Laodicea as a second water supply.

As we have seen with the other churches, this city was at the crossroads of trade. It was very proud of its position as the wealthiest city in the region due to its heavy finance and banking center. The valley had very fertile soil which was good for grazing sheep. The sheep were bred to produce soft, black wool. The black wool was not found in any other area, which put it in high demand.

There was a large, well established Jewish colony here before Christianity arrived. This provided a base for both the conversion to Christ and the rejection of Him. Interestingly enough, there were more slaves here than owners. At one point, there was an idea presented requiring the slaves to wear identifying clothing. After much discussion it was rejected because the slaves would realize there were more of them than the owners!

The same earthquake that destroyed, or damaged the other cities in 60 A.D. also destroyed Laodicea. However, due to their wealth, they rebuilt without needing assistance from the Roman government. This is another indicator of their wealth.

One of the main gods of this region was known as Men Karou. He was the god of healing, safety, fertility and the moon god. His image was that of a man with a crescent moon behind his shoulders. As the moon god, he was tied to the underworld as well; including the protection of the tombs.

On a side note, this church was the only one of the seven that Jesus found nothing good to say to them.

One group of people was known as the god-fearers. They were mainly gentiles who liked the Mosaic laws and traditions, but did not want to follow all of them, especially the wearing of long hair on the men and circumcision.

A medical school was near the temple to Men Karou on the outskirts of Laodicea. Once more we meet the god Asklepios who we met in Pergamum. His familiar snake wrapped around a pole was also present at this hospital.

What did John write to this church?

14 "And to the angel of the church of the Laodiceans write, 'These things says the Amen, the Faithful and True Witness, the Beginning of the creation of God:"

The term "Amen" is best defined by scripture, itself. We find in *2 Corinthians 1:20 "For all the promises of God in Him are Yes, and in Him Amen, to the glory of God through us."*

Jesus is the yes and Amen who has taught us by example how to give glory to His father, God.

Q How do I give glory to God? _____
_____
_____

Q How am I like this church? _____
_____
_____

15 "I know your works, that you are neither cold nor hot. I could wish you were cold or hot."

Known for being the "lukewarm" church, Laodicea drew its water from two sources. One was the hot mineral springs at Hierapolis, which flowed like a waterfall down the side of a mountain and across the valley. The other was the Lycus River which flowed six miles away, in the opposite direction.

Water from the hot springs had a nauseous odor and was full of minerals. The water was so concentrated that the Roman engineers created vent holes in the aqueduct pipes and covered them with stones, which could be removed so the pipes could be cleaned of the mineral buildup.

The water from the cold Lycus River would have lost its cool crisp flavor and become tasteless and lukewarm as it crossed the valley in terra cotta pipes. We see the hot springs and the cold river, but this is not what Jesus was talking about.

He was telling them they were lukewarm spiritually. He used those terms because the church knew those terms. Remember, Jesus talked in parables while He walked this earth. The people to whom He was addressing this letter would understand. They did not care about the importance of their spiritual walk, or for their maturity in the faith. They were lukewarm.

Q What are my "works?" _____
_____
_____

Q What can I do differently? _____
_____
_____

Q Am I lukewarm? _____
_____
_____

16 "So then, because you are lukewarm, and neither cold nor hot, I will vomit you out of My mouth."

Following through on the previous verse, we understand why He said He would vomit them out of His mouth. If you swallow something that tastes bad, you spit it out. In this case, the church was spiritually bad. They were not passionate in their walk and this was very distasteful to Him. Do you see that He is saying I "will" vomit you? He is not saying I "have" or I "am," in His loving way, He is still giving them a chance to turn back to Him.

Q Lord, help me to be "hot" for you. In order to do that, I know I need to _____
_____
_____

17 Because you say, 'I am rich, have become wealthy, and have need of nothing' - and do not know that you are wretched, miserable, poor, blind, and naked –"

Yes, in a worldly sense, they had become wealthy, very wealthy by mans standards. Remember, there was a great deal of commerce at this major crossroad. The finances and the selling of the black wool and textiles were only a few forms of wealth.

"Wretched:" the dictionary defines it as "of poor quality." They had chosen material wealth over spiritual wealth. In looking back at the other six churches, it is clear that Laodicea has fallen the farthest. Sadly, they see themselves as being the best!

"Miserable:" (some translations say pitiable) which the dictionary defines as "wretchedly unhappy or uncomfortable, pitiably small or inadequate." It appears Jesus wanted the people to see how far they had fallen.

"Poor:" Remember, this was a very wealthy city. They were quite proud of their financial and material "things." The men and women adorned themselves with expensive clothing and jewelry. Clothing we would wear for a very fancy event were common outfits here. Their homes also reflected wealth. To be called poor was a powerful insult, which Jesus knew they would understand because He was referring to their spiritual poverty.

"Blind:" is also a word they knew. In Laodicea there was a famous medical center. One of the main ailments was eye disease which was treated by creating a fine powder from a local stone (the Phrygian stone). It was mixed with oil and other ingredients; the eye was then washed with the mixture, producing great results for those afflicted. Yet Jesus told them they were blind. He, Jesus is the healing ointment, the eye wash for their spiritual lives. The only One who can open their spiritual eyes.

"Naked:" Laodicea was the fashion center. They took great pride in their dress, yet Jesus tells them they are naked. This is one more time He is speaking in a parable-like manner to them. They do have very nice clothes on, yet they are not clothed in Christ-like behavior. They are naked spiritually.

The church was so *"wretched, miserable, poor, blind, and naked"* that they could not even see their condition. It was impossible for the people to see how far they had fallen because they had allowed material things to take the place of spiritual maturity.

Q How does this church relate to modern times? _____
_____
_____

Q How does this relate to me? _____
_____
_____

18 "I counsel you to buy from Me gold refined in the fire, that you may be rich; and white garments, that you may be clothed, that the shame of your nakedness may not be revealed; and anoint your eyes with eye salve, that you may see."

This was a very wealthy city. They were used to buying and selling things for gold. Jesus is telling them to buy gold refined by Him so that they may be rich. Spiritually rich. He wants to develop a give-and-take relationship with them.

The popular fabric of the day was woven with golden threads. They wore it on a daily basis. Jesus tells them in verse 18 to buy white garments that they may be clothed, that the shame of their nakedness may not be revealed.

Throughout scripture, white garments represent the purity, righteousness and Holiness of Jesus. Spiritual nakedness is much more revealing than lack of clothes, and this group loved their clothes; yet were so naked on that most important spiritual level.

Once more He refers to the eye salve to heal their blindness. The eye wash should have been called "I" wash so they could cleanse their souls to see Christ in His greatness.

Q I know those people could not buy the white garments Jesus was referring to, neither can I. Jesus is telling me to: _____

_____

Q Do I have eyes, but do not see? _____

_____

19 "As many as I love, I rebuke and chasten. Therefore be zealous and repent."

It is clear that Jesus truly loved this church. How deeply He felt for their souls. He admits to rebuking and chastening them in anticipation of their repentance.

Q The next time I am going through a struggle, I know that He may be rebuking or chastening me. This is good for me because: __

_____

Q What do I need to do to repent? _____

_____

***20** "Behold, I stand at the door and knock. If anyone hears My voice and opens the door, I will come in to him and dine with him, and he with Me."*

We all know this verse. So, let's really learn it. Jesus is standing at the door of the church in Laodicea. He does not say He knocked and left, He said "I knock." That is a present tense statement. He is not banging, or beating. He was not lonely, looking for a friend; He was letting the church know that He was still outside.

Tradition says He is knocking on the door of our hearts, wanting us to invite Him in. We know that Jesus does want us to invite Him into our hearts, however there is nowhere in the Greek or Hebrew that refers to Him knocking at our heart in this verse. Modern commentaries do say He is knocking on the door of our hearts, but I could not find it anywhere in the original language. Having said that, we do know that the door to the heart, "the spiritual heart" is the door He wanted the church to open when they heard His knock.

If one reads each line of this verse carefully, He knocks, and then says "if anyone hears My voice and opens the door…"

He knocked on the door of the church in Laodicea, but what voice were they supposed to hear? They were ignoring the Holy Spirit! In this sentence, He was reminding the church that the heart cannot be open to the Holy Spirit until His voice is heard. Then and only then can He be invited in to dine with them. Sadly, few in this church wanted to hear His voice.

In modern European culture, the evening meal is where the

family gathers and lingers. This meal is not rushed, it is a time to visit, to tell of the day's events and simply enjoy each other's company. The Greek word for "dine" was *"deipnon."* The definition would be to eat a meal, yet linger, fellowship and spend intimate, personal time with each other for an extended period.

Jesus is saying he wants to spend quality time with them. He wants to recline amongst them and enjoy their company. In modern language, it would include "fellowshipping, or hanging out" together.

Q When Jesus knocks, am I ready to hear the Holy Spirit? _____
_____
_____

Q Am I ready to truly follow Him? _____
_____

Q How can I "dine" with Jesus each day? _____
_____
_____

21 To him who overcomes I will grant to sit with Me on My throne, as I also overcame and sat down with My Father on His throne.

This is a promise for those who chose to open that door and "deipnon" with their Lord. They will be welcome in heaven, not just heaven, but on His throne in heaven! A confirmation of this is found in 2 *Timothy 2:12 "If we endure, We shall also reign with Him. If we deny Him, He also will deny us."*

Q What makes me think I will sit with Him on His throne? _____
_____
_____

Q What have I done to deserve it? _____
_____
_____

Q Jesus said He overcame. Then he was able to sit down with His Father on His throne. What exactly did Jesus do to "overcome?"
_____
_____

22 *"He who has an ear, let him hear what the Spirit says to the churches."*

We have read this phrase at the end of each of the letters to the other 6 churches. This one is particularly interesting because the medical center which we studied regarding the eye was also famous for healing ear infections. The same stone; the Phrygian stone was ground to powder and mixed with other ingredients. The ear was then washed with the liquid producing a healing for the afflicted person.

Yet here, Jesus is speaking to them once more in terms they understood. They had ears that could hear, but they did not choose to hear what the Spirit was saying to their church.

Q How good is my hearing? My spiritual hearing? _____
_____
_____

Q What is my biggest take-away from this study? _____
_____
_____
_____

Temple to Athena

Temple to Athena in the foreground, columns for the Agora are behind.

EXPLORING THE SEVEN CHURCHES OF REVELATION

Excavation of entryway into a temple court

Modern Cross above an older carving of a Menorah on a white marble column.

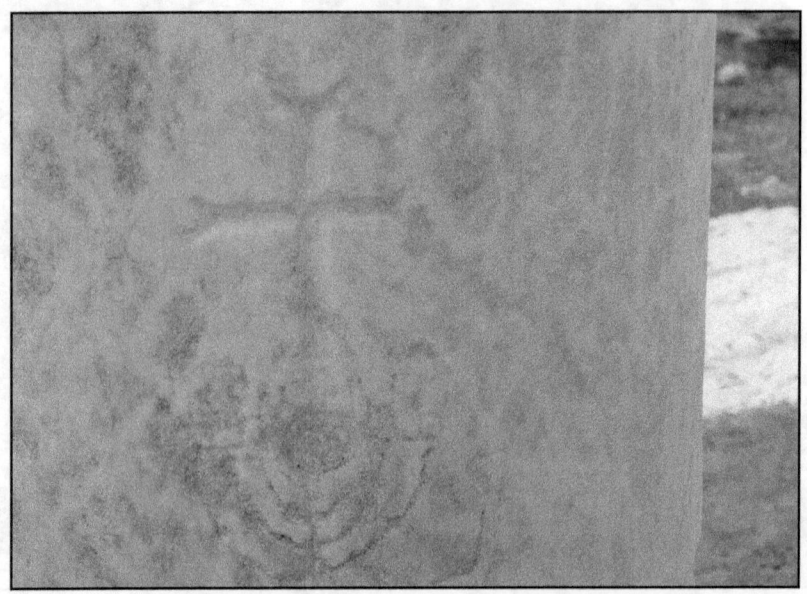

EXPLORING THE SEVEN CHURCHES OF REVELATION

I pray you will find a new and closer relationship with our Lord Jesus Christ.

HE simply wants your heart!

May God continue to shower blessings

upon you as you learn to

trust Him

more each day.

To place your order, Contact:

www.susanchowell.com

210-308-8500

10939 Wilson Oaks Drive

San Antonio, Texas 78249

www.ingramcontent.com/pod-product-compliance
Lightning Source LLC
Chambersburg PA
CBHW050603300426
44112CB00013B/2056